Gita Wisdom Tales

Dhyana–Meditation

Inspiring stories explaining the key shlokas of the Bhagavad Gita

Gauranga Darshan Das

Author's Note

Among all the scriptures, the Bhagavad Gita holds a special significance since these are the words of Lord Krishna who voiced the Gita at the onset of the Mahabharata war to motivate His dear friend and devotee, Arjuna. The Gita presents the truths of life with deep wisdom.

While sharing the Bhagavad Gita especially with children, I found the concepts of the Gita sinking in better when presented with suitable stories. I have, therefore, attempted to incorporate them in the *Gita Wisdom Tales* series in five volumes.

The intriguing anecdotes and examples infused in the book richen its flavour and open up a totally new dimension of the Gita to children and adults alike. These stories collected from various scriptures including the Srimad Bhagavatam, the Ramayana, the Mahabharata, the Puranas, and even some traditional folklore, highlight the import of 50 Bhagavad Gita shlokas in simple language. Along with these tales, the Gita wisdom will surely find its way into little hearts, and hearts that live young.

- Gauranga Darshan Das

Contents

Introduction: The Story of the Bhagavad Gita

Dear children! Do you know what the words 'Bhagavad Gita' mean? 'Bhagavan' means God. 'Gita' means a song. Therefore, Bhagavad Gita means the song that God has sung. Read on to know when, where, and why did God sing this divine song.

Dhritarashtra and Pandu were princes of the great empire of Hastinapur. Dhritarashtra was the elder brother. Since he was blind, Pandu became the king. Pandu had five noble sons named Yudhishthira, Bhima, Arjuna, Nakula and Sahadeva. Together they were known as the Pandavas. Dhritarashtra had one hundred sons, the eldest of them being the wicked Duryodhana.

Duryodhana hated the Pandavas and tried to kill them in many ways. He set their home on fire. He took away their kingdom by cheating in a dice game. He sent them on exile for thirteen years. Even after the Pandavas completed their period of exile, Duryodhana didn't return their kingdom. So, war between them became inevitable.

Finally, the armies of Yudhishthira and Duryodhana met on the battlefield at a place called Kurukshetra. Lord Krishna, the dearest friend and guide of the Pandavas, chose to steer the chariot of Arjuna during the battle. The war was about to begin.

Arjuna took up his bow but did not have the heart to shoot the arrows. He thought, *How can I kill my own relatives and friends? Isn't that sinful?* He softened towards his cousins and other family members. He was confused whether he should fight, or simply give up. He gave several reasons to Krishna why he could not fight. He placed his bow and arrows aside and sat down on his chariot saying, "Krishna, I shall not fight." Seeing His dear friend Arjuna immersed in deep confusion, Krishna tried motivating him. To clear the confusions in Arjuna's mind, Lord Krishna voiced the Bhagavad Gita.

Sometimes, we also get confused in our lives while performing our duties. The Gita takes us on a journey from confusion to clarity.

Although the Gita was narrated in the context of war, there was hardly any discussion about war in the Gita. The Gita presents several lessons on how to lead a meaningful life. Through Arjuna, Lord Krishna passed on His divine teachings to humankind. So let us read the beautiful Bhagavad Gita, God's message to all of us. This book presents some key shlokas, explained with suitable stories. Hope these wisdom tales will inspire you to read the entire Gita, when you are older.

1. HEARING OF HIS GLORY INCREASES LOVE

मय्यासक्तमनाः पार्थ योगं युञ्जन्मदाश्रयः ।
असंशयं समग्रं मां यथा ज्ञास्यसि तच्छृणु ॥

mayyasakta-manah partha
yogam yunjan mad-ashrayah
asamsayam samagram mam
yatha jnasyasi tat shrunu ॥ 7.1 ॥

Our attraction towards anyone is aroused when we hear good things about them. The more we hear their praises, the more we develop a love for them. The same is the case with God.

In this shloka Krishna says, " By hearing about Me, and thus being conscious of Me and taking My shelter, you can understand Me."

Read the story of Rukmini who fell in love with Krishna simply by hearing His praises.

Rukmini Desires to Marry Krishna

Princess Rukmini was the daughter of King Bhishmaka of Vidarbha. She had heard abundant praises of Krishna from sages like Narada. She thus fell in love with Him and desired Krishna as her husband. But her brother Rukmi wanted to marry her off to his evil friend Sishupal. Helpless, Rukmini wrote a letter to Krishna and sent it to Him through her trusted aide.

The letter read: *O Lord, I have heard Your praises and am attracted to You. I can marry no one else. My brother has arranged my marriage with Sishupal whom I hate. On my wedding day, I shall visit the temple of Ambika. Please take me from there along with You. I will not be able to live without You.*

Krishna and the aide at once set out for Vidarbha on His chariot, at the speed of wind. Meanwhile, Rukmini was anxiously waiting for Him. When she was informed of Krishna's arrival, her joy knew no bounds.

She happily went to pray at the temple of Ambika. It was the custom for the bride to pray at the temple before marriage. As she slowly walked out of the temple, she saw Krishna waiting for her. Then leaving everyone aghast, Krishna pulled her in His chariot and swiftly rode away.

All the envious kings including Jarasandha, Sishupal and Rukmi chased Krishna with their weapons and armies. Observing the sudden outset of such a war, Rukmini became fearful. But Krishna defeated all of them. However, Rukmi continued to chase Krishna hoping to get his sister back.

As Rukmi attacked Krishna with arrows, Krishna broke all his weapons to pieces, and raised His sword to kill him. But kind-hearted Rukmini requested Krishna to spare her brother's life. So, Krishna didn't kill Rukmi, but shaved off bits of his hair here and there, giving him a ridiculous haircut.

Then Lord Krishna took Rukmini to Dwarka where He married her and they lived happily together. In this way Rukmini fell in love with Krishna simply by hearing about Him and eventually became His first glorious queen.

Enthusiastic hearing about God sows the seed of love for Him within the heart.

Simple-hearted Devotion

Once in Vrindavan, little Krishna went out for a long stroll along with His gopa friends for herding His dear cows. On the way, the boys became hungry and requested Krishna and Balarama to do something.

Krishna told them, "Just nearby are some brahmanas who are performing a yagna for piety. You may go to them and ask for some food." The gopas at once went to the brahmanas, and requested for some food. But the brahmanas completely ignored them. The boys disappointedly returned to Krishna empty-handed.

Smiling slightly, Krishna then told them to approach the wives of the brahmanas with the same request, after informing them that He was hungry. The gopas followed Krishna's instruction. Having heard about Krishna's wonderful qualities, the wives of the brahmanas had always been eager to see Him.

The simple women immediately grabbed many fine foods and sweets and ran towards Krishna just as rivers flow towards the sea. When they reached the bank of River Yamuna, they saw Krishna dressed like a dramatic dancer, resting one hand upon His friend's shoulder and twirling a lotus with His other hand. The fortunate ladies embraced Krishna within their hearts.

Krishna welcomed them respectfully and said, "O great ladies, fortunate people like you serve Me selflessly, considering Me as the dearest." Krishna accepted their offerings, thanked them and told them to return to their homes. The ladies replied, "O Lord, please do not ask us to go back. We wish to remain in the forest serving You. We have already given up our homes. We have no shelter other than You."

Krishna replied, "You can worship Me perfectly by always thinking of Me, hearing about Me and discussing about Me. By doing so, very soon you will attain Me. Please go back." Accepting Krishna's words, the simple women returned home.

The brahmanas came to their senses and regretted their offence to Krishna. Seeing their wives' pure devotion, they condemned themselves, "Our high birth, learning, aristocracy and expertise in rituals is worthless. We are bewildered by Maya. The bhakti of our wives is rare. Although they did not undergo any Vedic processes like us, they have firm devotion for Lord Krishna. Though we had heard that the Supreme Lord appeared in the Yadu dynasty, we failed to recognise Him. Let us offer obeisances to Krishna and beg for His forgiveness."

Love for Krishna develops by hearing, chanting and worshipping Him, not necessarily by physical closeness.

Rukmini and the brahmana women developed a love for Krishna simply by hearing about Him. Therefore, by hearing about the Lord from the devotees and scriptures, we organically meditate on Him, and become eager to see Him, talk to Him, and establish a relationship with Him.

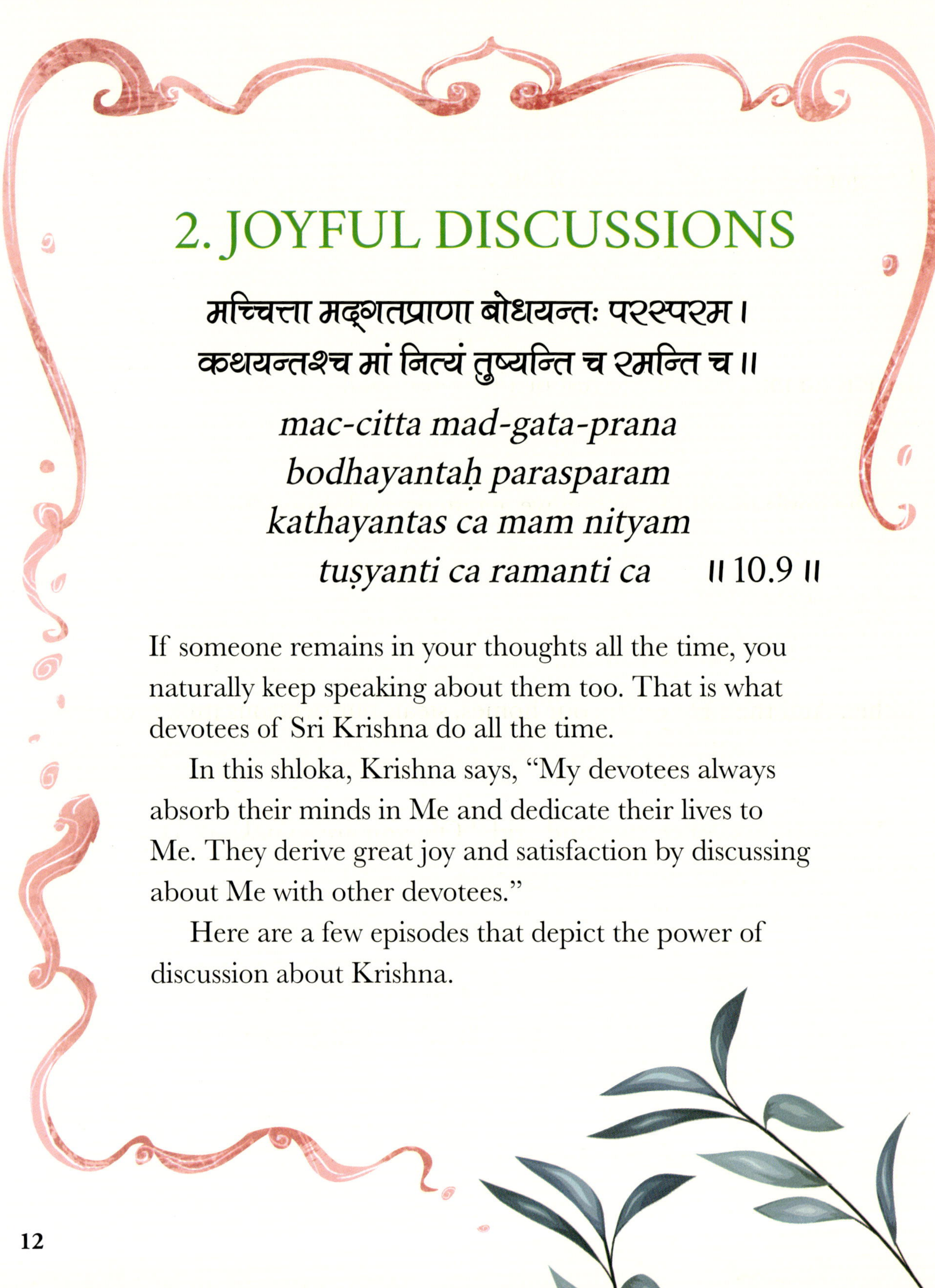

2. JOYFUL DISCUSSIONS

मच्चित्ता मद्गतप्राणा बोधयन्तः परस्परम् ।
कथयन्तश्च मां नित्यं तुष्यन्ति च रमन्ति च ॥

mac-citta mad-gata-prana
bodhayantaḥ parasparam
kathayantas ca mam nityam
tuṣyanti ca ramanti ca ॥ 10.9 ॥

If someone remains in your thoughts all the time, you naturally keep speaking about them too. That is what devotees of Sri Krishna do all the time.

In this shloka, Krishna says, "My devotees always absorb their minds in Me and dedicate their lives to Me. They derive great joy and satisfaction by discussing about Me with other devotees."

Here are a few episodes that depict the power of discussion about Krishna.

Loving Complaints

The gopis of Vrindavan were filled with joy on seeing Little Krishna's pranks and loved to discuss and meditate on them all the time. Although they delighted in them, they pretended to scold Him. Once they went to Mother Yashoda to lodge a complaint about how Krishna releases the calves in the shed who drink up all the milk of the mother cows and there is no milk left for the rest of the household.

Mother Yashoda spoke in His defense, "Krishna is just a child. He does this innocently. Why don't you stop Him?"

The gopis retorted, "When we get angry and shout, 'Beat Him, tie Him up…' He merely smiles. Smitten by His enchanting smile, we become speechless."

Yashoda asked in wonder, "But, why does He release the calves at all?"

The gopis said, "By releasing the calves, He make us run hither and thither. And then He enters our homes, steals our delicious milk products and eats them right in front of our eyes. He doesn't even pretend to run away. Yet, we are unable to do anything."

Yashoda was concerned and said, "Oh, you are so unkind! Why don't you give Him some milk before he takes it by Himself? He must be hungry."

The gopis responded, "No, it's not that He is hungry . His belly is always full since He is always being fed by you. He just loves to steal. He wants stolen milk only, and not the milk which we give Him. If we give Him milk, He refuses to drink it."

Yashoda argued, "It is not possible for an innocent child to steal from you. You are too clever for Him."

The gopis scoffed, “Innocent!? Your son is uncannily intelligent. He has invented innovative methods of stealing that are unseen or unheard of. He is a skillful stealer.” Yashoda tried to reason with them. “This is the result of the piety of your ancestors that Krishna is enjoying at your homes. Why don’t you accept this joyfully?”

“We are happy if He eats our butter, even with His friends. But He gives it to the monkeys. When the monkeys stop eating after their bellies are overfull, He breaks our pots saying that our butter is so bad that even monkeys refuse to eat it,” the gopis complained.

Yashoda gave them a look of disbelief.

In this way, there was no end to the

complaints of the gopis about Krishna. Sometimes, Mother Yashoda would defend Krishna, while at others, she would chastise Him in order to discipline and teach Him good manners. That was her absorption in her mood as the mother of Krishna, the Supreme God acting as the Supreme Thief.

If Krishna is God, why should He steal? Those were simply His playful pastimes as a child to attract our minds. By stealing butter, Krishna was actually stealing the pure butter-like hearts of the gopis. He was not hungry for milk, but was hungry for their motherly love. In fact, the gopis prepared all kinds of milk products only because they wanted Krishna to come and steal them.

These simple gopis were very appreciative of Mother Yashoda's fortune in being Krishna's mother. But they thought she must be bereft of the pleasure of witnessing Krishna's stealing pastimes, for He wouldn't steal butter in her house. So, in order to share the same joy with Yashoda, the gopis would narrate Krishna's stealing pastimes to her in the form of complaints.

The gopis' angry complaints were nothing but expressions of their love for Krishna, the Supreme butter thief (*makhanchor*) who steals the hearts of one and all.

Discussions about the Lord's activities and qualities are most enjoyable.

When God Hears About Himself

Lord Krishna spent His childhood in Vrindavan and performed sweet pastimes along with His elder brother Balarama which were witnessed by their mothers Yashoda and Rohini in Vrindavan as well.

After Krishna grew up, He shifted to Mathura and later to Dwarka, and married 16,108 queens. While in Dwarka, even in front of his queens, Lord Krishna would often remember His beloved friends in Vrindavan.

One day, Krishna's queens asked Balarama's mother Rohini, to tell them about Krishna's naughty activities in Vrindavan. Mother Rohini agreed, and all of them sat down in a big room to listen. They closed all the windows of the room. Rohini asked Krishna's sister, Subhadra to stand guard at the door and prevent Krishna and Balarama from entering the room.

Remembering her dear friend Yashoda, Rohini then began to speak about Krishna's wonderful pastimes in

Vrindavan. She described how the residents of Vrindavan identified Krishna as an innocent, naughty boy, son, friend, lover, and not as God. She described Krishna's simple attire in Vrindavan. As a cowherd boy, He would wear peacock feathers and play His flute. He loved and was loved by all the gopas and the gopis. The queens were satisfied and absorbed in hearing Mother Rohini speak. Subhadra at the door also became very curious to hear. So, she peeped into the room and listened. She became oblivious of the ones who passed by.

Meanwhile, Lord Krishna and Lord Balaram arrived there and saw Subhadra. Curious, they too stood on the right and left sides of their dear sister, and started overhearing Mother Rohini's wonderful stories.

Hearing about Their childhood, both Krishna and Balarama became overwhelmed with intense memories of Vrindavan. Krishna, Balarama and Subhadra became so absorbed in hearing, that Their hearts began to melt. They became so ecstatic that Their eyes became bigger and wider in amazement. Their heads compressed into their bodies. Their arms, legs, and neck also withdrew into Their bodies.

At that time, Narada Muni also happened to come by. Krishna was so blissful that He told him to ask for any boon that he wished. Narada then replied, "My Lord, may You three remain in those forms somewhere in this world and let the whole world see these blissful forms. That is what I want."

Granting Narada's wish, Krishna replied, "So be it! We will manifest in these forms in the city of Jagannath Puri, on the bank of the ocean." Thus, the beautiful forms of Jagannath, Baladeva and Subhadra manifested in Puri as a result of the bliss the Lord experienced while hearing His own pastimes.

God's pastimes are so sweet that He himself gets attracted to them.

Simply by discussing Krishna's pastimes, the motherly gopis of Vrindavan were full of love for Krishna. Mother Rohini filled the hearts of Krishna, Balarama and Subhadra with boundless joy. If we too narrate and share with our friends and family the sweet pastimes of Krishna, we too can experience unbounded happiness and satisfaction.

3. THE PROVIDER AND THE PROTECTOR

अनन्याश्चिन्तयन्तो मां ये जनाः पर्युपासते ।
तेषां नित्याभियुक्तानां योगक्षेमं वहाम्यहम् ॥

ananyas cintayanto mam
ye janah paryupasate
tesham nityabhiyuktanam
yoga-kshemam vahamy aham ॥ (9.22) ॥

Just as a mother never considers the child in her lap a burden, the Lord also personally maintains His devotees who always think of Him with love.

In this shloka, Krishna promises, "I love My devotees who always worship Me and meditate on Me without deviation. I will protect what they have (yoga), and provide what they need (*kshemam*). I will personally carry (*vahamy aham*) the burden of their maintenance."

Once, a thought came to the mind of a great devotee, *Why should Krishna personally carry what the devotees need*? How do you think Krishna dealt with him? Read the story to find.

The Divine Boys

Arjunacharya was a great brahmana devotee of Krishna. He lived with his wife in a small hut. Every day, he would beg for food to maintain his little family. He was poor, but scholarly. He would also read the Bhagavad Gita daily, and explain the shlokas nicely in his commentary.

One day, he was writing his commentary on the shloka given above, 'ananyas cintayanto mam…'. He thought, *How could the Lord say*, *vahamy aham – I will personally carry*? Arjunacharya therefore scratched out the word 'vahami' (I carry) and inserted 'karomi' (I get it done through someone). Having made that change, he went out to beg, as usual.

In the meanwhile, two attractive boys knocked at the door of Arjunacharya's house. His wife opened the door and saw two pleasant boys, one dark and one fair in complexion. They carried on their shoulders a huge quantity of food—rice, vegetables, fruits, butter, and so on. They insisted, "O mother, please accept this food." They were anxious to leave as early as possible. She asked them, "Who are you? Who has sent this?" They replied, "We are Arjunacharya's students. You husband has sent these items. Please take them quickly. Otherwise, your husband will beat us again."

Arjunacharya's wife was happy that she could cook some food for her hungry husband. But she couldn't believe that he would punish children who had such sweet faces. She told them, "My husband is not so cruel as to beat little boys." Then the dark boy turned around and showed her the marks on his back where he had been struck. He said, "See? Your husband makes us do hard work and when he becomes angry, he punishes us in this way."

Arjunacharya's wife was shocked. She invited the boys into her hutment and lovingly applied some sandalwood paste on the boy's back to relieve him of the pain. Then, the two boys left. She then cooked a meal with the ingredients the boys brought, and started eating.

Meanwhile, Arjunacharya returned, empty-handed. Because he had gone out to beg late that day, he couldn't get anything. Seeing his wife eating, he was surprised. She never ate before him. She would eat only after she had fed him lovingly. But today was different. She also looked very upset and neglectful. She didn't want to speak to him.

Arjunacharya asked her, "What's the reason for your strange behaviour today? Have I hurt you in some way?" She replied, "Not me! You have hurt small children. You have become so cruel." Arjunacharya replied, "I have never done so. Why would I do such a thing?" She then narrated what had happened when Arjunacharya was away.

Arjunacharya thought for a few moments and asked her, "What did the boys look like?" She replied, "One was darkish and the other was fair." He then understood. "It was Krishna and Balarama who came to our house. We are fortunate and blessed to have their darshan. The marks on the dark boy's back were a result of my scratching out the word *vahami*. Krishna had come personally to prove His words true. I was foolish, I couldn't trust His words." Arjunacharya was now completely convinced beyond any doubt that Krishna is the Supreme Provider and Protector of His devotees.

Krishna doesn't give a false promise. So, let us trust His words.

From Rags to Riches

Lord Krishna had a childhood friend named Sudama. Both of them studied in the same gurukul, under the guidance of the same guru, Sandipani Muni. Sudama was a poor brahmana. He used to maintain his family with whatever little came his way.

One day, Sudama's wife asked him to visit his friend Krishna in Dwarka and beg for some charity. Sudama didn't want to do so, but finally agreed when his wife insisted.

Sudama's wife begged a few handfuls of flat rice from her neighbours. She tied the rice in a torn cloth and gave it to Sudama to offer it as a gift to Krishna. Soon, Sudama reached Dwarka and stood before Krishna's palace.

Krishna stood up from His throne and joyfully ran to welcome him. Krishna hugged Sudama. Then, after offering him a comfortable seat, He respectfully washed Sudama's feet and sprinkled that water on His own head as a gesture of respect. He worshipped Sudama with incense, burning oil lamps, and so on, and showered him with many gifts while Rukmini kept fanning him. All the people in the palace were astonished to see how Krishna treated His poor friend.

Thereafter, Krishna eagerly asked Sudama if he had brought any gift for Him. Sudama was ashamed to offer his gift of begged, uncooked, flat rice. But Krishna grabbed the bundle that Sudama was hiding, and ate a handful of it with great joy. When He was about to eat another morsel, Rukmini lovingly stopped Him. She and the other queens also wanted a share.

Sudama spent that night comfortably in Krishna's palace, and set off for home the next morning, without asking for any favours from Krishna. But omniscient Krishna knew the reason behind Sudama's visit although He didn't speak of it to Sudama.

On his way back home, Sudama thought of his good fortune of being honoured by Krishna. He felt grateful for Krishna's loving treatment. When he reached home, to his surprise, he found a grand palace in place of his rundown hut. He saw his wife, adorned with expensive jewellery, coming out of the palace. She lovingly welcomed him. Sudama understood that it was Lord Krishna's mercy and entered his new 'home'.

Krishna values even the most insignificant gift of a devotee if it's simply offered with love.

Both Arjunacharya and Sudama naturally loved Krishna. So, Krishna understood their needs even before they could express them. One who always thinks of the Lord naturally attracts His grace and support. His loving protection is the hope of all the devotees.

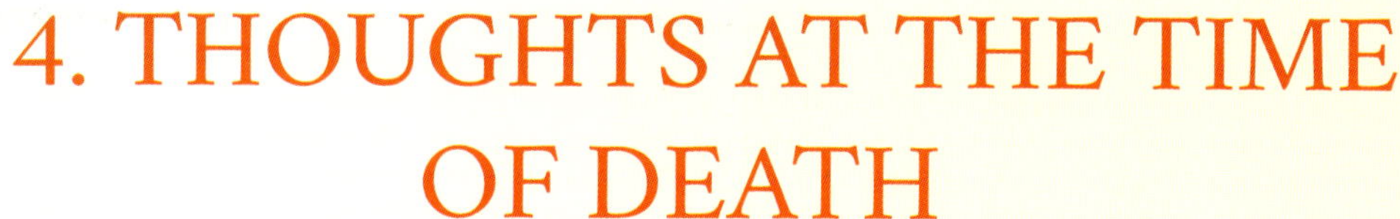

4. THOUGHTS AT THE TIME OF DEATH

यं यं वापि स्मरन्भावं त्यजत्यन्ते कलेवरम् ।
तं तमेवैति कौन्तेय सदा तद्भावभावितः ॥

yam yam vapi smaran bhavam
tyajatyante kalevaram
tam tam evaiti kaunteya
sada tad-bhava-bhavitah ॥ (8.6) ॥

We often hear that, "Life is a preparation, and death is an examination". Doesn't our performance in an exam depend on our study and revision before the exam? It is our performance in the final exam that decides our promotion to the next grade. Similarly, one's actions and thoughts throughout one's life makes one think of something at the time of death, and thus attain that form in the next life. Let's understand this better with the help of the following stories.

Do you know what one becomes in the next life? Lord Krishna answers in this shloka: "Whatever one thinks of at the time of death, he attains that form."

The King Who Became a Deer

King Bharat was a great king who performed various sacrifices as worship unto Lord Vishnu. After ruling the Earth for 10,000,000 years, he divided his wealth among his five sons and renounced the kingdom.

Bharat then went to a peaceful place called Pulahashram, where the river Gandhaki flowed. There, Bharat built a small hermitage and lived alone. He would bathe in the river and worship Lord Vishnu with various flowers, Tulasi leaves, and water from the river. His heart was completely satisfied with such selfless worship of the Lord.

Once, while sitting on the bank of the river, Bharat began to chant some prayers. At that time, a thirsty, pregnant doe happened to come by. As she started drinking water from the river peacefully, she suddenly

heard the roar of a lion. Scared, she quickly leapt away, although her thirst was still unquenched. When she thus leapt in fear, her baby fell from her womb into the flowing waters. The distresssed doe died on the spot.

Seeing the new-born fawn floating down the river, Bharat felt great compassion. He immediately lifted it from the water. Knowing the fawn to be motherless, he brought it to his hermitage. He began to raise the helpless animal as his child. However, by being so absorbed in caring for the fawn, he gradually neglected his worship unto Lord Vishnu.

Due to his excessive affection Bharat lay down, walked about, bathed, and even ate with the fawn. Fearing that ferocious animals might kill it, Bharat took it with him wherever he went in the forest. He would carry the fawn on his shoulders, sometimes placed it on his lap or, when sleeping, on his chest.

Once, the fawn wandered into the forest, alone. Not being able to find it, Bharat became as anxious as a miser who loses his wealth. King Bharat, who was once immersed in the thoughts of Lord Vishnu, now became immersed in the thoughts of the lost fawn.

He thought, *Oh, I am so negligent and cruel like a hunter. Perhaps the deer lost faith in me and left me. Oh, shall I ever see it again? Will the Lord protect the deer? When will I see him wandering again in the garden, eating the soft grass?*

Seeing the dark marks on the rising moon that resembled the fawn, he said, "Has the compassionate moon given it shelter? Is the moon protecting it from the fearful attacks of a lion?" Unfortunately, Bharat was overwhelmed by an intense desire to see the fawn and forgot his spiritual goals.

Bharat's thoughts about the fawn increased with time, and his life span decreased. Finally, the time of death approached him. Absorbed in thoughts of the fawn while leaving his body, Bharat died. He was born as a deer in his next life, in the region of the Kalanjara Mountain.

But, by the Lord's grace, he remembered his past life even in the body of a deer. He thus meditated on the Lord, and was born as a brahmana in his next life, and finally attained the Lord by remembering Him.

Our emotions and attachments shouldn't distract us from our goals.

Some More Time, Please!

Once there lived a man named Kailash. He was a disciple of the great sage, Narada Muni. One day, Narada Muni told him, "It's time for you to become serious in spiritual life and worship the Lord." Kailash said, “My dear Gurudev, I know this. But my children are still young. Let them grow up and complete their education. Then I shall perform bhakti more seriously.”

Some years later, Narada Muni met Kailash once again and asked, “Kailash, now your children are grown up. You need to really take shelter of Lord Krishna.” Kailash replied, “I know, but my children are still not married. Let me just get them married.”

In a few years, all his children got married, and Narada Muni returned to him. But Kailash explained, “Dear Gurudev! I need to really make my business flourish and save enough money for my children’s future. Please give me some more time.” Seeing Kailash so deeply absorbed in the thoughts of his family, and fully attached to his home, Narada Muni pitied him and went away.

After some years, the sage came back and spoke to Kailash, “Now your children are married, and they are capable enough to take care of their financial needs. It’s time for you to become serious in bhakti.”

Kailash replied, “I am sorry, Gurudev. My

children are not very experienced in business. They need my guidance. Also, I have my grandsons to take care of. Please give me some more time."

Narada Muni went back, and came after a few years. But he didn't find Kailash at his home. He enquired from Kailash's children, "Where is your father?" They replied, "O Sage, our father has recently died."

Hearing this, Narada Muni started walking away. Then he heard a dog barking. Narada Muni saw the dog. The dog said, "O Sage! It's me, Kailash." Because of his attachment to his home and family, Kailash was born as a dog at the same place.

Narada Muni saw him and mercifully replied, "Oh! You have become a dog! Still, it's not too late. Come with me now. Take shelter of the Lord." The dog replied, "I am sorry, Narada Muni, I have acquired a lot of wealth and built this house in my human life. But my sons are very careless. They are not taking care of the property properly. I have to protect it from thieves. Please come back later." Pitying Kailash for being still so attached to the home and family of his past life, Narada went away.

After some years, Narada came back but the dog wasn't there. Upon inquiry, he learnt that the dog was dead. Hearing this, Narada started walking out, when he heard the hissing of a snake. Narada turned back, and the snake spoke, "Gurudev! It's me, Kailash!"

Because Kailash as a dog always thought about his past house and family, he was born as a snake near that very house.

Narada told him, "What are you doing here, Kailash?

You can still come with me. Take shelter of the Lord." The snake replied, "Dear Narada, my children and grandchildren are not taking care of the fields. They are lazy and wake up late in the morning. By that time all the grains and vegetables in the field are stolen by the neighbours. Therefore, I have become a snake to protect the field from thieves. I am very busy now. I am sorry. I cannot come with you."

This time, Narada Muni didn't go back. He went into the house and told the people, "A poisonous snake is near your house!" Then the sons and grandsons of Kailash came there with sticks. Narada showed them the large snake (Kailash), and they immediately started beating it with sticks.

Kailash in his snake body hissed and tried explaining to his sons that he was their father. But the more he hissed, the more his sons beat him. Then Kailash spoke to Narada Muni, "O Gurudev, It's time! Now is the time for me to take bhakti seriously. I shall come with you. I shall take shelter of Lord Krishna."

Bharat always thought of the deer and became a deer in the next life while Kailash always thought about his home and family and was repeatedly born near that home. Instead of thinking of something temporary, if one thinks of God, one will attain the kingdom of God after death. Interesting, isn't it? Let's read the next shloka and the stories that follow to know more.

It's not worthy to always think of temporary attachments and postpone spiritual life.

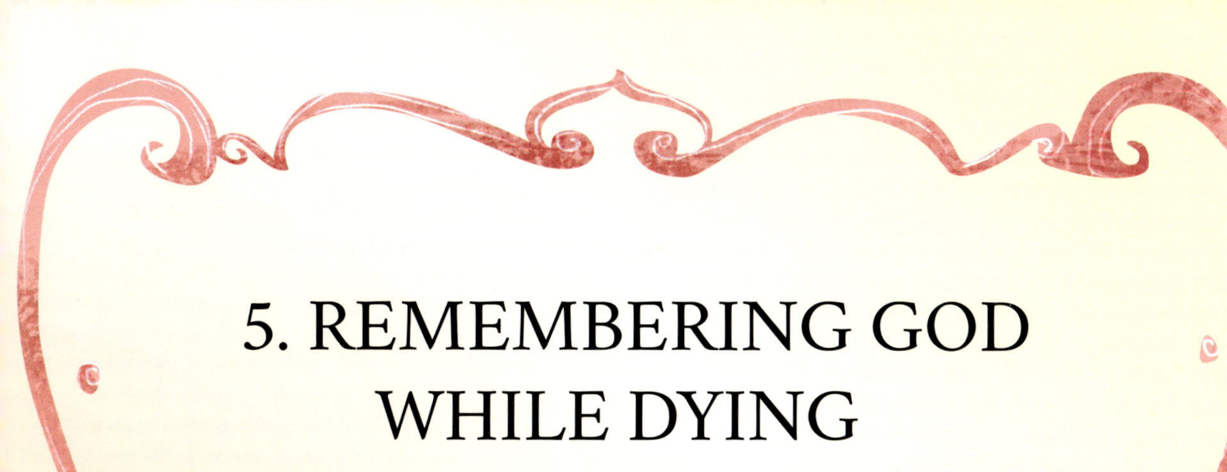

5. REMEMBERING GOD WHILE DYING

अन्तकाले च मामेव स्मरन्मुक्त्वा कलेवरम् ।
यः प्रयाति स मद्भावं याति नास्त्यत्र संशय ॥

anta-kale ca mam eva
smaran muktva kalevaram
yah prayati sa mad-bhavam
yati nasty atra samsayah ॥ 8.5 ॥

We know from the previous shloka that if one thinks of something at the time of death, one attains that form. But what if one thinks of God while dying?

In this shloka, Krishna says, "Whoever remembers Me at the time of death undoubtedly reaches Me." This is the way of attaining the kingdom of God.

But how can one remember Krishna at the time of death? By constantly practising to think of Krishna during our lifetime. Here are two thrilling stories for you to relish and ponder upon.

Dying on a Bed of Arrows

Bhishma was the illustrious grandfather of the Kuru dynasty. He was a great devotee of Lord Krishna. Bhishma's father Shantanu had given him a special boon of 'iccha-mrityu' meaning Bhishma would die only when he wished to.

Bhishma loved the Pandavas and protected them in various ways. He was virtuous and vastly learned but he had to fight on the side of Duryodhana against the Pandavas, in the Kurukshetra battle. It was because Lord Krishna wanted to teach the world an important lesson through Bhishma that vice cannot conquer virtue regardless of who tries to execute it. In the battle of Kurukshetra, Arjuna shot several arrows that pierced the entire body of Bhishma who then fell down on the ground. Soon the battle was over and the Pandavas emerged victorious.

Meanwhile, Bhishma lay down in the battlefield on a bed of arrows. He had always wanted to see the Pandavas happy and prosperous.

But because of wicked Duryodhana and his associates, the Pandavas underwent a lot of hardships. Now that the Pandavas had regained the kingdom, Krishna brought them before Bhishma to make him happy as he lay on his deathbed.

With teary eyes, Bhishma spoke to the Pandavas, "Please rule the kingdom and take care of the people responsibly. This is the wish of Lord Krishna. Although Krishna is equal for everyone, He is specially inclined to His pure devotees. Therefore, He has mercifully come before me now at the last stage of my life."

At that time, the auspicious time of uttarayana had arrived. Bhishma decided to leave his body. He withdrew his mind from everything else, and focussed only on Lord Krishna, who stood near him in a four-handed form, which was Bhishma's favourite.

Bhishma offered his prayers to the Lord, "Let me offer Him the gift of my loving thoughts and emotions. His glittering form shines in the Sun, and curly locks of hair surround His lotus face. Let my mind go unto Sri Krishna on the battlefield, as the chariot driver of Arjuna. His flowing hair is covered with the dust raised by the horses, and His face is drenched in sweat."

Thus, meditating on Krishna, Bhishma left his body and entered one of the Vaikunttha planets, where the Lord is in His eternal form. Celebrating this event, the devatas praised Bhishma and showered flowers from the sky. Then, Yudhishthira performed the funeral rites for the departed Bhishma. Thus, Krishna mercifully gave His darshan to His devotee Bhishma at the time of his death.

Thoughts about the Lord lead one towards the Lord.

Ajamila Chants 'Narayana'

Ajamila was a learned brahmana from a place called Kanyakubja. He was respectful and kind towards everyone, and had no bad qualities. However, Ajamila got deviated from the path of devotion because of wilfully associating with a a lady of questionable character. He gave up his parents, good wife and good manners. He started indulging in sins like drinking, stealing, cheating, and so on. He spent eighty-eight years of his life in this manner.

Ajamila had ten sons. He named his youngest son 'Narayana' who was very dear to his parents. Old Ajamila took great pleasure in Narayana's innocent prattle and childlike activities. With deep affection, Ajamila would often call out, 'Narayana, Narayana' repeatedly. Whenever he sat down to eat, he would call out to the child, "Narayana, come and sit, eat this food." When he would drink, he would call, "Narayana, come and drink this juice."

Years passed and gradually old age caught up with Ajamila. When he was on his deathbed, he saw three terrifying persons approaching him. They were the Yamadutas, the soldiers of Lord Yama, who would give suitable punishments to sinful people in hell. Ajamila had committed unlimited sins with his body, mind, and words. Therefore, three Yamadutas came to him with ropes to drag him to hell.

Frightened, with tears in his eyes, Ajamila loudly called his son, 'Narayana, Narayana,' who was playing nearby. Unfortunately, the boy didn't have the maturity to understand his father's plight. But even though the child 'Narayana' didn't respond to Ajamila's cries, Lord Narayana did. Ajamila had neglected the worship of Lord Narayana all these days, but the Lord's heart melted hearing him helplessly call out His name. The Lord mercifully sent His servants, the Vishnudutas, to rescue him. Because dying Ajamila chanted four syllables 'Na-ra-ya-na', four effulgent Vishnudutas came to rescue him.

As the Yamadutas were snatching the soul from the core of Ajamila's heart, the Vishnudutas stopped them. They looked very fresh and beautiful in silk garments. Their faces were glowing with lotus-like eyes and dazzling crowns. Their four long arms held maces, bows, quivers of arrows, swords, clubs, conches, chakras and lotus flowers. They were also decorated with lotus garlands and jewellery. Their effulgence dissipated all darkness. For they are capable of punishing anyone, including Yama, if they wrong a devotee of Vishnu.

The Vishnudutas told the Yamadutas, "Ajamila helplessly chanted the name of Lord Narayana while on his deathbed. Earlier, whenever Ajamila called out to his son, he uttered the holy name of Narayana affectionately. Even unintentional and unconscious chanting of the Lord's name destroys all sins. Therefore, do not take Ajamila to hell. As a fire burns dry grass to ashes, the Lord's holy name whether chanted knowingly or unknowingly, burns the sin of wicked acts. Just as a powerful medicine acts even when taken without the knowledge of its powers, the Lord's holy name is effective even when the chanter utters it unknowingly."

The Vishnudutas cut the ropes of the Yamadutas and sent them away. Ajamila bowed his head at the feet of the Vishnudutas. Then, as he was about to say something, the Vishnudutas suddenly disappeared.

Ajamila was saved from death and being sent to hell. He repented for his sinful life, "Alas, I have led a sinful life. Having gotten this second chance, I will give up my sinful habits, and perform bhakti unto Lord Narayana, and chant His names with love and affection."

Ajamila then went to a holy place called Haridwar, where he performed bhakti with full dedication. After thus living a purely spiritual life for twelve years, Ajamila gave up his material body on the banks of the River Ganges and attained a spiritual body appropriate to that of a devotee of Lord Vishnu. A golden *vimaana* from Vaikunttha arrived to gloriously carry Ajamila back to Lord Vishnu.

God is always merciful to His devotees, even if they sometimes commit mistakes.

Lord Krishna personally came to Bhishma at the time of his death, and sent him to the spiritual world. Lord Narayana sent His servants to save Ajamila who chanted 'Narayana' while he actually called out to his son. In this way, the Lord is always kind towards anyone who intentionally or unintentionally takes His shelter. Thus, let us consciously and constantly meditate on the Lord with love and finally reach Him.

6. ABSORPTION IN SERVICE

मन्मना भव मद्भक्तो मद्याजी मां नमस्कुरु ।
मामेवैष्यसि सत्यं ते प्रतिजाने प्रियोऽसि मे ॥

man-mana bhava mad-bhakto
mad-yaji mam namaskuru
mam evaishyasi satyam te
pratijane priyo 'si me ॥ 18.65 ॥

What are the best ways to connect with God? In this shloka, Lord Krishna gives us four simple ways to reach Him: "Always think of Me, become My devotee, worship Me, and offer obeisances to Me. By doing so, you will surely come to Me. I promise you, for you are very dear to Me."

One who takes to these four simple activities can easily attain the Lord's loving protection either in this world or in the spiritual world. Let's read about devotees who absorbed themselves in the Lord in these four ways, and finally attained Him.

The Cure to a Snakebite

Once, there lived a great devotee of Lord Venkateshwara (Balaji) in the holy place of Tirupati. His name was Anantacharya. He was a disciple of the great saint Sripad Ramanujacharya from South India. He was well-known for his wonderful service of growing fragrant flowers for the Lord's worship.

One day, Anantacharya was plucking Tulasi leaves in the garden to make a garland for Lord Venkateshwara. Suddenly, a poisonous cobra bit his leg. But Anantacharya remained fearless. Paying no attention to the snake's bite, he went on plucking flowers for Lord Balaji's service. He was always confident of the Lord's protection, so there was no reason for him to fear.

The disciples of Anantacharya noticed this, and were horrified that their Guru had just been bitten by a cobra. They immediately approached him and said, "Dear Guru Dev, you need treatment now. Please allow us to find a doctor and get you some medicine. The snake's poison is spreading and rising throughout your body." But Anantacharya dismissed their suggestions and continued his service.

The confused disciples went to Lord Venkateshwara's deity in the temple and prayed, "O Lord, our Guru was bitten by a cobra. Please advise him to see a doctor and take some medicine. We are worried about him."

Worried about His devotee's condition, the deity of Lord Balaji directly spoke to Anantacharya, "My dear Ananta, you were bitten by a venomous cobra. There is deadly poison spreading in your body. Please take the antidote quickly."

With folded hands, Anantacharya replied to the Lord, "My dear Lord, I am completely pleased and satisfied to take your extraordinary darshan. But O Lord, which poison are you talking about? I have two kinds of poison within me. One poison consists of my bad qualities like ego, pride, greed and anger while the other one is the snake's. The snake's poison can only harm my body, but not the soul. But the poison of ego and greed can terribly harm the soul. So which poison should I pay more attention to? The poison of ego and greed cannot be cured by any doctor of this world. It can only be cured by Your mercy. Therefore, I take your complete shelter, only by serving You."

The Lord replied, "My beloved Ananta, you are very dear to Me. I will be greatly pained if you die. I will miss the fragrant flowers that you grow for Me. Please take the antidote quickly."

Anantacharya replied, "O Lord, I am like a venomous snake filled with poison. But if the snake's poison is more powerful than mine, I shall die. If I live, I will bathe in Swami Pushkarini in the Tirumala hill and lovingly serve You in Your deity form of Venkateshwara. But if I die, I will take my bath in the Viraja River at the entrance of Vaikunttha, and I will see You and heartily serve You in Vaikunttha. Therefore, O Lord, whether I live or die, I will carry on my service to you by offering Tulasi and flowers for I am always your eternal servant."

Lord Venkateshwara was deeply pleased and impressed with the simple and unflinching devotion of Anantacharya. By the Lord's grace, Anantacharya survived the snakebite, and continued with his wonderful service to Lord Balaji.

Devotees are undisturbed by any danger to themselves due to their absorption in the Lord's service.

Cooking Sweet Rice in Meditation

In the city of Pratisthanapur in South India lived a poor brahmana. He thought he was poor due to his past sins. Thus, he was not sorry for his poor situation, but was always peaceful and satisfied with what he had. The brahmana was very interested in hearing about God. He would regularly go to spiritual meetings where great devotees lectured about the Lord.

One day, he went to a spiritual discourse by a great devotee. There the speaker said, "If one cannot directly worship the Lord with expensive dresses, ornaments, garlands, and food, one can do so even by meditation, and acquire the same results."

The simple brahmana thought, *Because of my poverty, I am unable to serve Lord Vishnu opulently. I do not have money to purchase expensive clothes, flowers, fruits and food items to offer to the Lord. But this idea is really good. Let me simply meditate on serving the Lord grandly and royally.* He thus started mediating.

He bathed in the holy River Godavari. After that, he sat down in a clean place on the bank of the river and started meditating on the Lord's beautiful form and service. In his meditation, he started dressing the Lord with colourful clothes, glittering ornaments and a dazzling crown. Then bowing down before the Lord with great devotion, he began to imagine that he was cleaning the Lord's temple. He carried water from the river in big vessels made of gold and silver. Not only did he collect water from the Godavari, but also from rivers Ganga, Yamuna, Narmada and Kaveri. Then he collected many fragrant flowers, ripe fruits, sweet incense and sandalwood pulp and brought them before the deity of Lord Vishnu. He offered all these items to the

Lord with great devotion and satisfaction. Then he offered arati and an elaborate feast to the Lord. In this way, the brahmana would daily worship the Lord in his meditation. He did so for countless years.

One day, he was cooking sweet rice for the Lord in his meditation. He got the best milk, sugar and ghee, and cooked with great care. When the sweet rice was ready, he waited for it to cool down. The cooler the sweet rice, the better it tastes. To check how hot the sweet rice was, he dipped his finger in the cooking pot and immediately burnt his finger for it was still hot. This broke his meditation.

Coming out of his meditation, the brahmana looked at his finger. His finger was actually burnt! He was surprised and thought, *My worship, my cooking, and my touching the sweet rice was all done in a state of meditation. How is it then that my finger has actually burned*?

While he was thinking so, Lord Vishnu in Vaikunttha started laughing. Next to Him was Goddess Lakshmi. She was curious and asked Lord Vishnu the reason for His laughter. "My Lord, what happened? Why are You laughing?" The Lord did not reply, but instead called His *dootas* and said, "Go in the vimaana and bring that brahmana from Pratisthanapur here."

Immediately the dootas of the Lord went to that brahmana and asked him to sit in the vimaana. The brahmana was astonished. He went to Vaikunttha along with them and stood before Lord Vishnu. The Lord narrated the whole story to Lakshmi, and appreciated the brahmana's absorption in his service, even in meditation. The Lord made the brahmana eternally stay in Vaikunttha for his loving services.

The brahmana's happiness knew no bounds. He was fortunate enough to get an eternal place in Vaikunttha in the association of the Lord and Mother Lakshmi.

Although the Lord stays in the spiritual world, He is present everywhere and observes our activities. Being present in the heart of the brahmana, the Lord observed and accepted all his worship while he was meditating. Thus, because of the brahmana's constant absorption in his service, the Lord was pleased and gave the brahmana a place in Vaikunttha.

The Lord accepts anything we offer Him with love, even in meditation.

Both Anantacharya and the brahmana were great devotees who always absorbed themselves in thinking of the Lord, worshipping Him and offering obeisances to Him. In turn, the Lord reciprocated with both of them in unique ways. Let us also adapt the four simple activities suggested by Krishna in this shloka and reach Him easily.

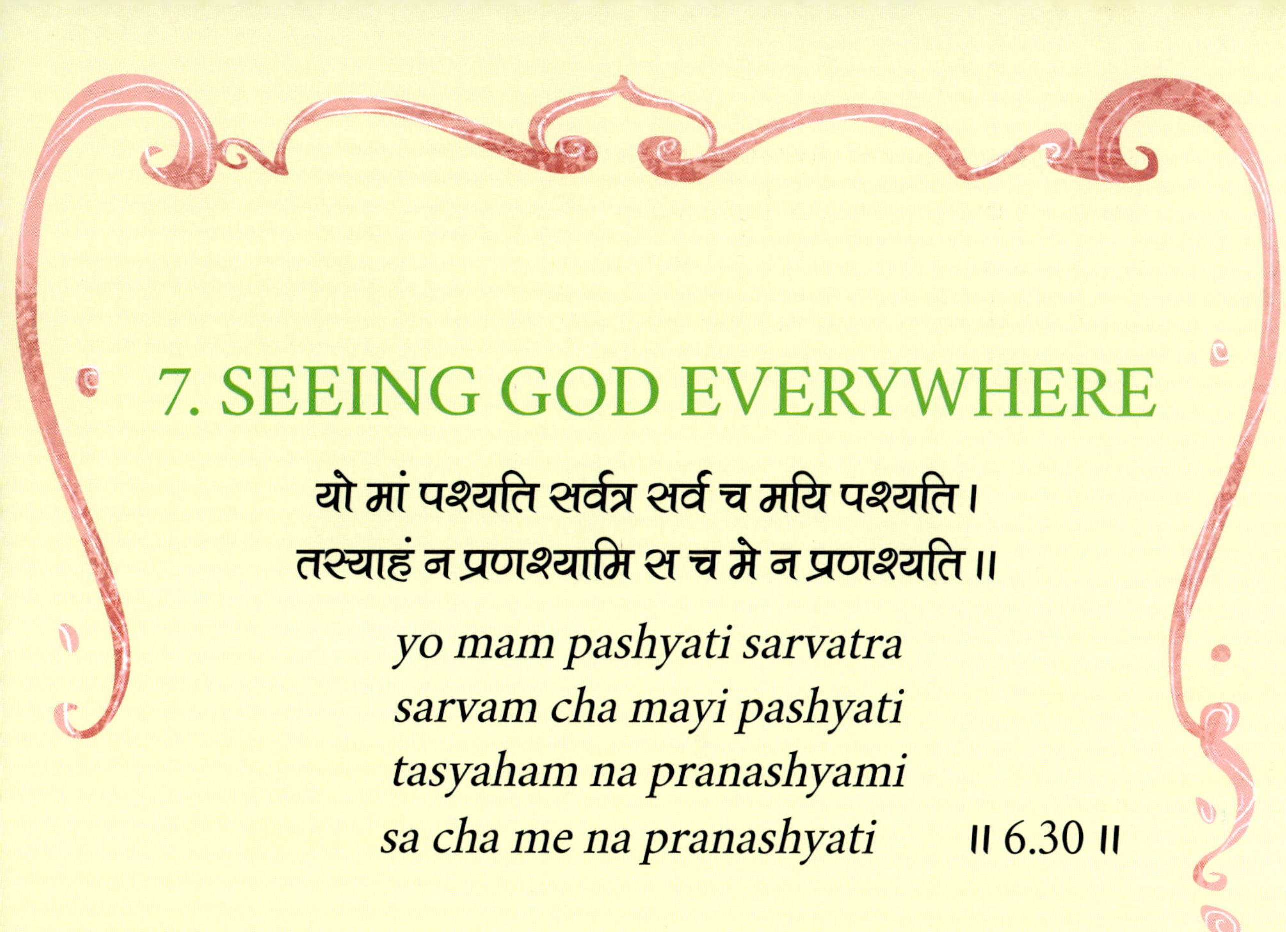

7. SEEING GOD EVERYWHERE

योमां पश्यति सर्वत्र सर्वं च मयि पश्यति ।
तस्याहं न प्रणश्यामि स च मे न प्रणश्यति ॥

yo mam pashyati sarvatra
sarvam cha mayi pashyati
tasyaham na pranashyami
sa cha me na pranashyati ॥ 6.30 ॥

If God is everywhere, why can't we see Him? One who has deep love for Him, firm faith in Him and thus constantly meditates on Him is the one who can see Him everywhere.

In this shloka, Krishna says, "My devotees see Me everywhere and see all things in Me. I am never lost to them, nor are they ever lost to Me."

Here are two stories of two young boys who saw the Lord everywhere.

The 'Inedible' Mango

One day, the Guru of a gurukul called his disciples and said, "My dear children, now I will give you a fruit each. I want you to eat this fruit in a place where no one sees you."

The disciples took the fruits and dispersed to different places to eat the fruits. After some time they all returned to the guru empty-handed.

The guru asked the disciples, "Where did each one of you eat your fruit?"

One boy replied, "I ate my fruit behind the tree."

Another boy said, "I ate the fruit below the cot."

Yet another boy said, "I entered the field behind the gurukul and ate it."

In this way all the boys found some secluded place where there was no one to see them, and ate the fruit.

But one boy still had the fruit in his hand. The guru asked that boy, "Oh, why are you still carrying this fruit?"

The boy replied, "My dear guru, I couldn't find a secluded place. Wherever I went, I found one person watching me. He was present in all directions. I couldn't find a single place where He was not present. Therefore, I couldn't fulfil the condition and thus, I brought it back."

The guru asked the disciple, "Who was that person?"

The boy replied, "It was Lord Krishna! In your Bhagavad-Gita class, you explained how Krishna is present everywhere, in every corner of the entire Universe. I saw Krishna wherever I went." The guru appreciated the boy's intelligence and devotion unto Lord Krishna. As the boy grew up, his devotion and meditation on the Lord also increased, and eventually he became a great devotee.

Although the Lord is everywhere, He is visible only to those who deeply love Him.

God in a Pillar

Hiranyakashipu was the king of the asuras. He had received boons from Lord Brahma and had become powerful. Soon, he started troubling the devas, sages and the innocent people. Hiranyakashipu had a five-year-old son named Prahlada who had started studying under the materialistic teachers, Shanda and Amarka.

One day, Hiranyakashipu wanted to test Prahlada's knowledge. He asked Prahlada, "My dear boy, please repeat what you have learnt from your teachers." Then Prahlada fearlessly spoke about bhakti unto Lord Vishnu. Hiranyakashipu became upset with this. He got angry at the teachers Shanda and Amarka, and rebuked Prahlada.

Enraged at little Prahlada's deep devotion to Lord Vishnu, the hard-hearted asura king wanted to kill the boy. He tried to kill Prahlada by tossing him under the feet of big elephants, stranding him among venomous snakes, employing destructive spells, hurling him from the top of a hill, imprisoning him, poisoning him, starving him, exposing him to severe cold, wind, fire and water, and releasing heavy stones to crush him.

Throughout these extreme abuses and mistreatments, Prahlada's devotion to Lord Vishnu didn't diminish even slightly. Further, he absolutely had no bitter feelings towards Hiranyakashipu.

Perplexed about how his five-year-old boy could be so fearless, Hiranyakashipu once asked Prahlada, "You know that when I am angry, all the planets along with their rulers begin to tremble. By whose power have you become so fearless that you dare to overstep my power?" Prahlada replied, "The source of my strength is the source of your strength too. That source, Lord Vishnu, is the original source of all kinds of strength for every single being."

Hiranyakshipu threatened to kill Prahlada, and challengingly asked him, "Is your God present in this pillar?"

Prahlada confidently replied, "Yes, my Lord is present everywhere."

Hiranyakashipu then struck the pillar in rage. To uphold the declaration of His devotee Prahlada, Lord Vishnu appeared from the pillar in a wonderful form as Nrisimhadeva. In the ferocious form of a half-man and half-lion, Nrisimhadeva killed Hiranyakashipu merely with His nails, and protected Prahlada. Being forgiving to everyone, naturally Prahlada requested the Lord to excuse his father's mistake, and the Lord happily granted his young devotee's wish.

One who fully trusts God sees Him everywhere and fears nothing.

The little boy who did not eat the fruit and Prahalad, both saw God everywhere. The Lord is everywhere, but owing to His spiritual form, we cannot see Him with our material eyes. But those who have deep love for the Lord can feel His presence always and everywhere. They can even personally see Him when their love for Him matures.

8. DEDICATED MIND AND INTELLIGENCE

मय्येव मन आधत्स्व मयि बुद्धिं निवेशय ।
निवसिष्यसि मय्येव अत ऊर्ध्वं न संशयः ॥

mayy eva mana adhatsva
mayi buddhim niveshaya
nivasishyasi mayy eva
ata urdhvam na sanshayah ॥ 12.8 ॥

Are there multiple ways of serving the Lord? Yes, we can serve Him with our body, mind and intelligence. In this shloka, Lord Krishna says, "Fix your mind on Me alone. Dedicate your intelligence to Me. Thus, you will always live in Me, undoubtedly."

There are many examples of great devotees who had deep loving emotions for the Lord. There are also devotees who served the Lord with their wonderful intelligence. Here are two stories for your inspiration.

Radha's Mind Absorbed in Krishna

Once, Lord Sri Krishna and Srimati Radharani were sitting together in Vrindavan. A bumblebee happened to come there and started buzzing around Radha's face. The bee saw Radha's reddish feet and mistaking them for a lotus flower, it kept humming and hovering around them. Radha became afraid of the bee.

Lord Krishna noticed this. He called his friend Madhumangal and requested, "Madhu, please chase this bee away, so that it never comes back."

Madhumangal was one of the dear friends of Krishna. He was very jovial and friendly in his behaviour and had great love for Krishna. When Krishna called Madhumangal, he immediately came there. With many humorous gestures, he playfully drove the bee away easily to a distant place.

He then came back to the place where Radha and Krishna were sitting, and reported, "Now Madhusudan is gone. He will never come back." Madhusudan means a bee, and it is also one of the names of Lord Krishna. Hearing Madhumangal's words, Radharani felt that Krishna had gone away, and thus she began to cry.

Radharani wept and repeatedly cried out, "O Krishna, the Lord of my life, where have You gone?" With her mind immersed in love for Krishna she intensely emoted and cried. But Krishna was present right next to her. Krishna tried to console her, "Radha, I am here, next to you. Please don't cry."

But the very thought of Krishna's going away from her made Radharani's mind weep. Such was her love for Krishna. Seeing Radharani's intense love for Him, tears began to well up in Krishna's eyes. He also joined Radharani as she continued crying. The mix of the tears of love of both Radha and Krishna formed a lake called the 'Prema Sarovar' which can still be found in Vrindavan.

The loving emotions of devotees melt the Lord's heart.

Hanuman's Intelligence in Rama's Service

During the war between Lord Rama and the demon Ravana, Rama and Lakshman killed many demons effortlessly. Rama had killed even the formidable Kumbhakarna, the brother of Ravana. Proud Ravana had never expected that a few human beings accompanied by some monkeys could terrorise his vast rakshasa army in such a way.

As Ravana sat on his golden throne, his son Indrajit approached him and said, "Dear father, why are you so sorrowful? These humans and monkeys will not survive my attacks. I shall tear them to pieces by my weapons today." With great hope, Ravana sent Indrajit to the battlefield with his great army.

Indrajit ordered his army to attack the monkeys with their sharp arrows and lances, and mystically remaining invisible, he killed the monkey army with his razor-headed arrows, lances and maces. With a single arrow he pierced as many as five, seven, or even a dozen monkeys. Yet, the monkeys who were dedicated to serve Lord Rama continued to fight.

Indrajit's arrows pierced the chief monkey heroes like Jambavan, Sugriva and Angada, and even Rama and Lakshman were completely covered with those arrows. Rama said to Lakshman, "This demon has released the *brahmastra* weapon, and has overpowered our army. We will also get affected by this." Then both the brothers fell to the ground and dropped Their bows.

Indrajit was joyful and considered Rama and Lakshman dead. He saw that only a few thousand monkeys remained on the battlefield. As the sun was setting, Indrajit returned to Lanka to deliver the good news to his father Ravana.

Mighty Hanuman and Vibhishan survived the attack of Indrajit. Hanuman looked around, and saw the chief warriors, including Rama and Lakshman lying on the ground, unconscious. He immediately ran to Rama and Lakshman and sat near Them. Tears rolled down his cheeks. Vibhishan placed his hand on Hanuman's shoulder, and spoke gently, "My dear friend, don't be despondent. Rama and Lakshman voluntarily fell unconscious just to honour the brahmastra. Indeed, They are virtue personified. They will surely rise and defeat Ravana's evil forces."

Hanuman then saw Jambavan lying there, and went to him. Jambavan said softly, "O Hanuman, only you can save this army. You must go to the Himalayas, and bring the four precious herbs, namely, *sanjivakarani* that brings a dead person back to life, *vishalyakarani* that heals all wounds, *sandhani* and *suvarnakarani* that can restore a wounded body. They all grow together atop the Himalayas. Please leave at once and bring them here."

Hanuman immediately stood up, expanded his body and shouted, "Victory to Rama!" He then soared through the sky, and finally reached the mountain where the celestial herbs grew. As he was searching for them, the herbs noticed that someone had come to take them and hid themselves. Those herbs, being divine, were only visible to the devatas and none other.

Hanuman looked for the herbs everywhere,

but couldn't find them. He was deeply concerned about Rama, Lakshmana, and the monkey army.

With his mighty hand, Hanuman then lifted the huge mountain peak with all its tigers, elephants, deer, and the herbs. Hanuman sprang into the air, and soared high into the sky. With the shining mountain peak in his hand, he looked like the blazing sun moving in the sky.

Hanuman soon arrived near Lanka and dropped to his knees by the side of Rama and Lakshmana. Then slowly, Rama breathed deeply, inhaling the celestial fragrance of the herbs. Gradually, He opened His lotus eyes. He saw Hanuman and smiled. Hanuman was relieved and his heart experienced great joy. Quickly he began administering the herbs to Lakshman, who also returned to consciousness.

With tears in His eyes, Rama hugged Hanuman and thanked him for his dedicated service. Later, Rama and Lakshman courageously fought and They easily defeated Ravana along with his wicked army.

How much we love God is seen in how much we extend ourselves in His service.

Srimati Radharani's mind couldn't bear the thought of being away from Krishna. Hanuman making use of his intelligence, brought the summit of the mountain, for he couldn't bear the sight of Lord Rama lying unconscious on the battlefield. By absorbing our mind and intelligence while serving the Lord, we can strengthen our relationship with Him.

9. REACHING GOD

जितात्मनः प्रशान्तस्य परमात्मा समाहितः ।
शीतोष्णसुखदुःखेषु तथा मानापमानयोः ॥

jitatmanaḥ prashantasya
paramatma samahitah
sitoshna-sukha-duhkheshu
tatha manapamanayoh ॥ 6.7 ॥

How can one overcome all obstacles and reach God? Krishna answers this question in the shloka given above which means, "One who controls the mind is peaceful, and remains unaffected by happiness and distress, heat and cold, honour and dishonour, can easily reach the Lord."

Here are the examples of two great personalities who exhibited the above qualities and finally attained the Lord, despite many difficulties on the path.

The Boy Who Saw Krishna in His Heart

Once there lived a poor woman. She had a five-year-old son, and no other relative. She was very fond of her son and wanted to look after all his needs as best as she could. The boy was also dependent on his mother's affection and never went anywhere, nor met anyone in her absence. He always believed that he would never be separated from his mother.

Once, some great sages called the *bhakti-vedantas* arrived at the house of the boy. They were learned in the Vedas and were sinless. They were great devotees of Lord Krishna. They decided to stay with the boy and his mother during the four months of the rainy season. The woman and her son served them in various ways.

Whenever the bhakti-vedantas discussed the appealing activities of Lord Krishna, the boy would attentively hear them. He was disciplined, humble, and obedient to elders. The sages were impressed with his conduct and blessed him.

Thus, during the two seasons—monsoon and autumn–the boy gradually became a wonderful devotee of Krishna. Before departing, the sages mercifully taught the boy Srimad Bhagavatam even though he didn't ask for it. They initiated him on the path of bhakti. After the sages left, the boy continued to live with his mother.

One day, an unexpected incident took place in the boy's life. His poor mother went out to milk a cow in the evening when she was bitten by a poisonous snake. She died instantly, and thus the boy lost his affectionate mother, his only caretaker, and was left alone in the world.

The boy was mature enough to see the hand of God even in this tragic incident. He thought, *The Lord is the Supreme well-wisher of His devotees. It is by His mercy alone by which I am put in this situation.* So, he decided to travel towards the north.

The boy passed alone through many cities, towns, villages, farms, mines, agricultural lands, valleys, forests, hills and mountains. He travelled through huge fearsome forests dense with reeds, cane, clumps of grass, and hollow bamboos, the playground for snakes, owls, and jackals. Still, he felt no fear, as he constantly depended on the Lord. He always meditated on the Lord and didn't waste even a single moment.

One day, he came upon a river filled with beautiful lotuses, surrounded by bees and singing birds. Tired and thirsty, he bathed in

the river, and drank some water. He was thus relieved from exhaustion. Then, sitting under the shade of a big banyan tree, he began to meditate upon Lord Krishna with great love. He fully concentrated his mind on Paramatma or the Supersoul situated within the heart, as taught to him by the sages.

While the boy meditated on the Lord with great emotion and love, tears fell from his eyes, and Lord Krishna appeared in his heart. The boy could experience the fragrance of Krishna's body, the sound of Krishna's ankle bells and the beauty of Krishna's face. He was thus absorbed in an ocean of joy as he experienced intense horripilation. Suddenly, he lost the vision of the Lord. He resumed meditating on the Lord with greater intensity, but couldn't see the Lord again.

Seeing his sincere endeavour, the Lord spoke to him, "My dear child, I showed Myself to you once, just to increase your desire to see Me more. Continue to meditate on Me and serve Me with devotion. You will soon become My associate in the spiritual world."

From then on, the boy repeatedly chanted the Lord's holy name. After giving up his mortal body, in his next life, he became the great Sage Narada with a spiritual body.

By sincere meditation, one can attain great blessings of the Lord.

Liberation of a Cow-killer

There was once a courageous prince named Prishadhra. His family priest was the great Sage Vashishttha. Although a qualified royal prince, Prishadhra took a vow to protect cows, following his guru's order. He would stand all night with a sword in hand to protect the cows from ferocious animals.

One night, a ferocious tiger entered the cowshed. All the cows ran here and there in fear. The tiger seized a cow, who mooed in distress. Outside, it was completely dark. The stars were covered by the clouds.

Prishadhra took up his sword and followed the sound of the cow in the darkness. He wanted to kill the tiger and save the cow. He approached the spot, but mistaking the cow for the tiger, he cut off the cow's head. Prishadhra didn't realise what he had just done.

In the morning, when Prishadhra saw that he had killed the cow, he felt extremely distressed and guilty. Cows are like a mother, and killing a cow is very sinful. Prishadhra never wanted to kill the cow. He was known for his service to cows, but he had accidentally ended up killing one.

The news reached Sage Vashishttha. Although Prishadhra's sin was unintentional, Vashishttha cursed him to be a low born man in the next life. Instead of relieving Prishadhra for his unintentional sin by some atonement, Vashishttha cursed him out of anger. Prishadhra didn't argue with the sage, but accepted the curse with folded hands. He then took the vow of brahmacharya and did not marry.

Thereafter, Prishadhra fixed his mind on Lord Vasudeva, with single-minded devotion. He became detached, peaceful, self-controlled, and satisfied with knowledge. He travelled over the Earth, while constantly meditating on the Lord with devotion, absorbed in pure bhakti. One day, he saw a forest fire and entered the fire. He thus attained Lord Vasudeva in the spiritual world. Because of his constant meditation and devotion for the Lord, Vashishttha's curse didn't affect him. Instead, he was liberated and attained the spiritual world.

One can even change one's destiny by devotion to God.

Both the boy and Prishadhra in the stories above demonstrated the qualities that Lord Krishna described in the shloka. They exercised mind control, were peaceful and unaffected by happiness and distress. Thus, they easily reached the Lord. Cultivating these qualities within us will ensure we reach Krishna.

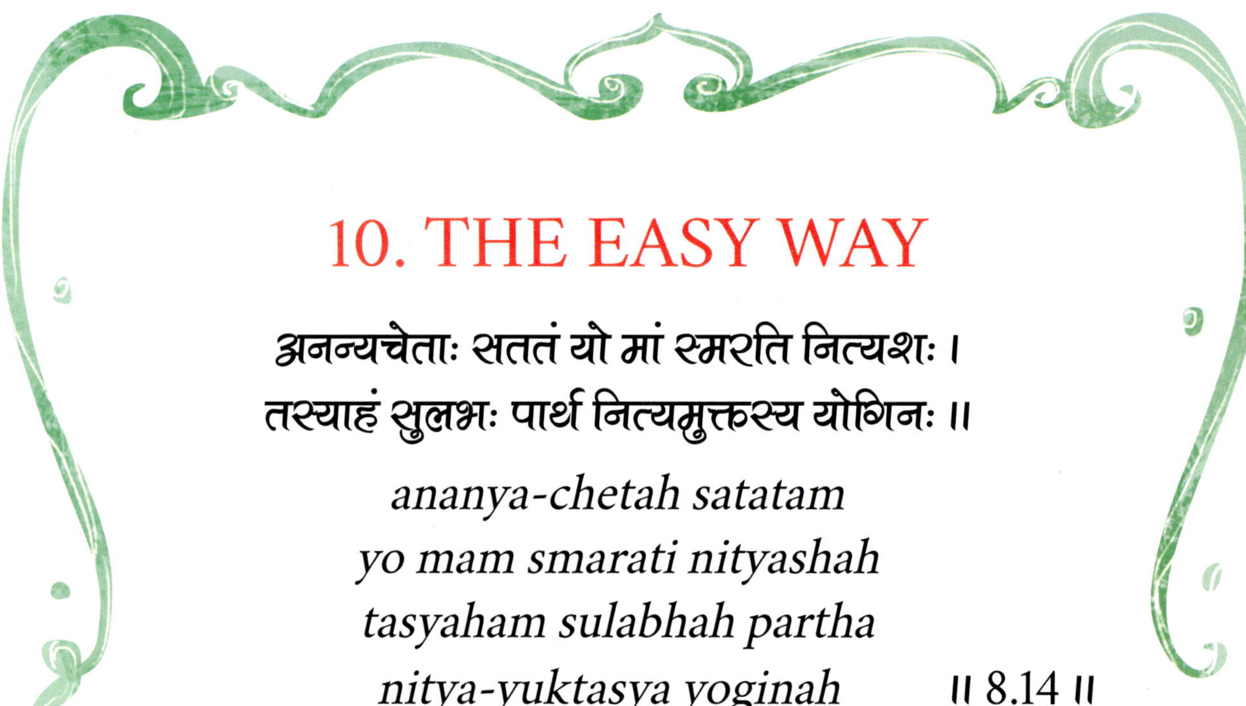

10. THE EASY WAY

अनन्यचेताः सततं यो मां स्मरति नित्यशः ।
तस्याहं सुलभः पार्थ नित्यमुक्तस्य योगिनः ॥

ananya-chetah satatam
yo mam smarati nityashah
tasyaham sulabhah partha
nitya-yuktasya yoginah ॥ 8.14 ॥

How difficult is it to please the Lord? Well, it depends on how far we are from serving Him with love and faith.

In this shloka Lord Krishna says, "Those who always think of Me with deep devotion, can easily (sulabha) attain Me, because of their constant absorption in Me."

In the entire Bhagavad Gita, Lord Krishna uses the word 'sulabha', meaning 'easy' only in this shloka. For those who have simple faith and devotion in the Lord, it becomes easy to attain His mercy, while for others it remains daunting. Here are the episodes of two great devotees who easily obtained the Lord's grace.

The Deity Who Ate All the Food

Mukund, a great devotee of Lord Gopinath(Krishna) daily worshipped his deity with great devotion. His son Raghunandan was five years old.

One day, Mukund had to urgently go out for some work, so he wanted Raghunandan to serve the deity of Gopinath that day. Entrusting the responsibility of the deity service to Raghunandan, Mukund went out.

Little Raghunandan collected the offerings to Lord Gopinath from his mother, and entered the deity room. He had seen his father offer food to the Lord earlier. He chanted some mantras, rang the bell, and waited for Lord Gopinath to eat the food. But the food remained on the plate, untouched.

Raghunandan was disappointed and worried. He thought that his father would be upset for having left the deity hungry. He repeatedly prayed to Gopinath with tears in his eyes, "O Lord, please eat the food! Please eat!"

Seeing the innocent boy in tears, Lord Gopinath spoke to him, "My dear child, why are your crying?" Raghunandan said, "Because you are not eating the food I offered."

Lord Gopinath replied, "I have already eaten."

Raghunandan questioned, "When did you eat my Lord? All the food is still on the plate. You haven't eaten. Please eat."

Lord Gopinath replied, "This is how I eat. I eat in a spiritual way, just by glancing at the food. Now the food on your plate is prasadam. You and your family can eat it."

Young Raghunandan didn't understand all that philosophy. He argued, "No, all the food is still here, untouched. Please eat it." Impressed with the loving appeal of the boy, Lord Gopinath ate all the food without leaving a single grain. Raghunandan gave the empty plate to his mother who thought that Raghunandan himself had eaten all the food. She was upset and waited for her husband's return.

When Mukund returned, Raghunandan joyfully told him, "Father, I have fed the Lord as per your instructions. He ate everything I offered Him."

Mukund was very curious to know about what had actually happened. He gave a laddu to Raghunandan and asked him to offer it to Gopinath. Raghunandan took the laddu and went to the deity. Mukund hid and secretly saw everything that was happening.

Raghunandan was very happy to serve Lord Gopinathji once again. Placing the laddu before Him, he prayed to Gopinath to eat it. Then, Gopinath extended His hand to pick up the laddu and started eating it. Mukund was astonished. Lord Gopinath was aware that He was being watched by Mukund. He ate one half of the laddu, and left the other half for He had eaten only a short while ago.

Mukund's eyes flooded with tears. He took his son on his lap and practically bathed him with the tears of his affection and joy. He felt fortunate to have such a pure devotee as his son.

The Lord is not hungry for our offerings, but He is hungry for our love.

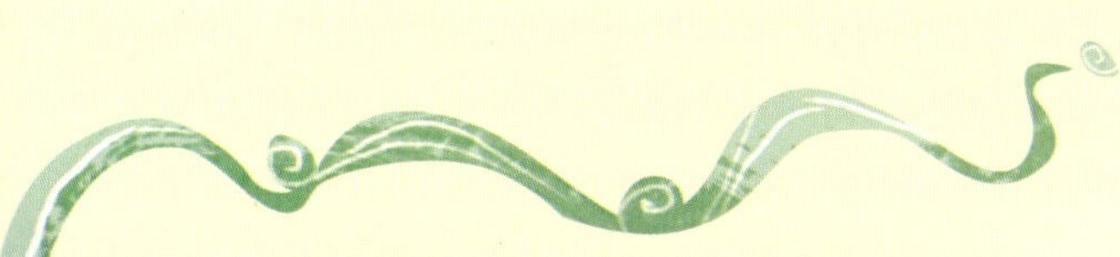

The Mystical Jewel

Once there lived a greedy man. He loved money and tried to acquire it in many ways. One day, he heard that a saint named Sanatan Goswami who lived in Vrindavan had a mystical stone called the Parasmani. Anyone who possessed it, would become as rich as he wished.

So the greedy man decided to somehow get that Parasmani for himself. He thought, *What will a sadhu do with the precious stone? I must have it.*

He went to Sanatan Goswami and said, "Dear saint, Please can you give me the mystical stone?"

Sanatan Goswami said, "Sure, please take it. It's lying there in that garbage."

The man wondered, *Parasmani in garbage*? *In such a dirty place*!

Nevertheless, he went to the garbage and started shuffling through it in great eagerness and greed. Finally he found the Parasmani, which was covered with dirt.

The man generated a lot of gold and became very rich, famous and powerful. But he was not satisfied. He had no peace.

He thought to himself, *I have all kinds of possessions. I'm still not happy. But Sanatan Goswami is still very happy and peaceful. He must be having something better than Parasmani that's making him happy. Otherwise, why would he keep it in a garbage dump? Why would he easily give it to me? I must go and ask him, and get his secret treasure.*

So he went back to Vrindavan and met Sanatan Goswami once again and asked, "O great saint, why did you keep the Parasmani in the garbage? You never used it. Do you have something more valuable than this?"

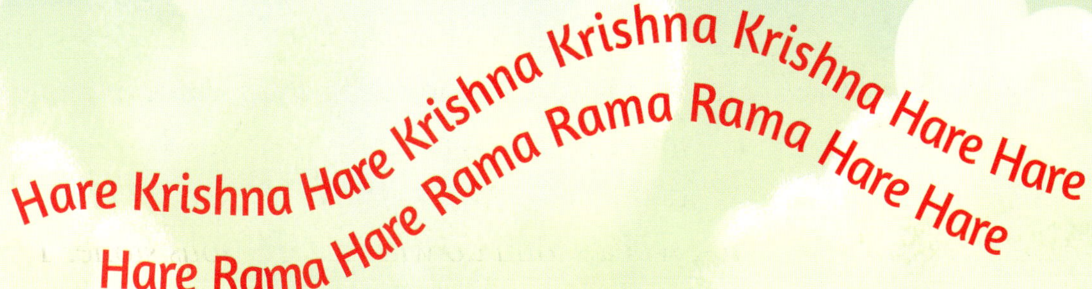
Hare Krishna Hare Krishna Krishna Krishna Hare Hare
Hare Rama Hare Rama Rama Rama Hare Hare

Sanatan Goswami replied, "Yes! I have something that is millions of times more valuable than this insignificant Parasmani."

The man eagerly replied, "I want it. Please give that to me."

Sanatan Goswami said, "I'll give it to you but first you must throw the Parasmani in the River Yamuna."

The man thought, *If I throw this in the Yamuna it'll be gone forever. But I am going to get something more valuable.* Thinking thus, he threw it in the Yamuna.

He came back to Sanatan Goswami and said, "I have given up the most valuable thing I ever had in my whole life—the Parasmani. Now please give me the best thing you have."

Sanatan Goswami said, "Yes! I'll now give you the supreme wealth which will give you the ultimate happiness. Please sit here and listen carefully–*'Hare Krishna Hare Krishna Krishna Krishna Hare Hare, Hare Rama Hare Rama Rama Rama Hare Hare.'* This mahamantra is the most precious wealth. I derive great happiness only from this. By chanting this mantra, we develop love for the Lord and reach Him beyond this temporary material world. It easily gives us the supreme spiritual joy." The greedy man now understood what real wealth is, and started chanting the names of the Lord and meditated on the Lord. He then attained that permanent happiness which all his wealth and gold couldn't give him.

The Lord's name is the wealth that provides utmost joy. Raghunandan expected the Lord to physically eat the food he offered Him, and the Lord easily responded to his innocent appeal. Sanatan Goswami taught us that real joy is easily attained by chanting the Lord's names. Thus one who connects with the Lord with love can easily get His mercy.

The Power of Dhyana–Meditation

From the stories of the Inedible Mango to The Mystical Jewel, one thing is clear. Once we invite Lord Krishna into our minds through devotional meditation, He will be happy to remain with us forever!

The more we think of God , the more we can feel His presence around us, and always within us. These stories can be narrated to family and friends and help spread the love of God.

Our next volume contains more exciting and fulfilling stories on Sadguna—Virtue. So, see you there!

– Gauranga Darshan Das

Author's Profile

Gauranga Darshan Das, a disciple of His Holiness Radhanath Swami, is a distinguished educator, and spiritual author of over 30 books. He holds a Master's degree from the prestigious Indian Institute of Science (IISc), Bangalore, India.

In his current role as the Dean of Bhaktivedanta Vidyapitha at ISKCON Govardhan Ecovillage (GEV), Gauranga Darshan Das conducts spiritual education programs in both residential and online platforms. He is a prolific speaker and teacher, renowned for presenting timeless wisdom in a lucid and contemporary form to various audiences, including children, teens, professionals and educators. He travels to various places in India, Australia, United States, etc., to share wisdom in various forums including temples, ashrams, schools, colleges, and the corporate sector.

He has lectured over 7,500 hours and conducted over 50 online courses (www.vidyapitha.in).

As an accomplished author, he has penned more than 30 books, including study guides (the *Subodhini* series), storybooks, self-enrichment works (*Dhruva*, etc.), and children's literature (*Bhagavatam Tales, Gita Wisdom Tales* series). He runs a monthly ezine called *Bhagavata Pradipika* whilst penning thought-inspiring articles for international and Indian *Back to Godhead* magazines. His dedication to the dissemination of spiritual wisdom has made him a respected figure in spiritual, educational, and corporate circles.

Know more about him on www.gaurangadarshan.com